MW01489309

Table of Contents

ABOUT THE AUTHOR

MAN MAN'S WINGS OF DREAMs

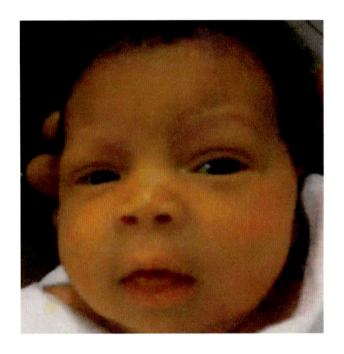

INSPIRATION

DICATION

This heartfelt revelation resonated deeply with Nana, sparking a resolute commitment to wholeheartedly support his aspirations. She regales him with accounts of legendary pilots and inventive geniuses, filling his young mind with inspiration and a sense of purpose.

One sun-drenched
After a deeply moving conversation in the afternoon, Nana came to a transformative realization. During the conversation, Man-Man inquired about Nana's relationship with his father. She understood the profound importance of cultivating a Meaningful relationship with Man-Man, a bond transcending past misunderstandings.

This story encapsulates the essence of familial love, reconciliation, and the boundless spirit of adventure.

INTRODUCTION

A New Adventure Armed with curiosity; Nana began learning about Airplanes from Man-Man.

Together, they explored aviation books and watched documentaries, with Man-Man eager to share his knowledge about airplane models and their intricate Parts.

Nana's Airplane Journey Nana marveled at how much Man-Man knew how enthusiastic he was. He became her little professor, teaching her the mighty machines that soared through the Skies.

Together, they would make airplane models, dreaming of a day when they would visit an air show or even a real plane cockpit.

A Twist in the Tale One day, Man-Man expressed another interest— security cameras. "Nana," he asked, "could you get me some cameras for my room? Nana, intrigued, asked what he planned to do with them. With excitement gleaming, Man-Man replied, "I want to create my own security system.

Empowering Dreams Seeing potential in his innovative spirit, Nana supported his new interest.

They researched together, learned how cameras worked, and even set up a simple system for Man Man's room. His creative solutions and technical curiosity amazed Nana.

Conclusion: A Legacy of Support Through their adventures with airplanes and cameras, Nana and Man-Man built a strong, loving bond. Nana learned to appreciate Man Man's unique talents and interests, realizing that nurturing his passions could shape a bright future.

Together, they shared dreams of the skies and gadgets, with Nana always encouraging Man-Man to soar high and explore fearlessly. Reflection: on a journey from misunderstandings to shared dreams, Nana found that the best way to mend hearts and inspire young minds is through patience, understanding, and a willingness to learn together. As their bond grew stronger, Nana and Man-Man ventured into new horizons, exploring the intricate world of technology and innovation

.

They attended workshops, visited museums and joined community clubs where Man-Man could showcase his talents. Nana found herself a guardian and a student in the fascinating universe her grandson was unraveling.
Man-Man's confidence soared as he realized he had a partner in his grandmother, who believed in his dreams and encouraged his curiosity.

Their journey was not just about learning facts and building gadgets but about creating memories and A legacy of mutual respect and love that would last a lifetime.

Through every project and discovery, Nana and Man-Man exemplified how true connection, and understanding could transform life and inspire endless possibilities.

Amidst life's challenges, she discovered profound comfort in the deep connections she cultivated with her family, diligently fostering affection and comprehension. These hard-won life lessons formed the bedrock of the wisdom she now imparted to Man-Man.

Their shared enthusiasm blossomed into a bond far exceeding the conventional grandparent-grandchild relationship; it evolved into a genuine collaborative quest for knowledge.

Their days reverberated with the joy of discovery, from the marvels of flight dynamics to the intricacies of observation technology – a symphony of experimentation and mirth.

Nana's unwavering encouragement and Man-Man's insatiable curiosity propelled their shared explorations, creating a haven of mutual respect and understanding.

Their journey exemplified the incredible power of shared admiration and a thirst for knowledge, forging a future where aspirations weren't mere fantasies, but attainable objectives nourished by a legacy of steadfast support and boundless inquisitiveness.

Man-Man, his eyes alight with wonder, hung on her every word. He confided his fervent ambition to Become an aerospace engineer and craft aircraft capable of reshaping the world.

This heartfelt revelation resonated deeply with his youthful mind, inspiration, and a profound sense of purpose.

Exploring Interests

Eager to connect, Nana asked Man-Man about his interests. When he passionately shared his fascination with airplanes, Nana. Their days were filled with shared discoveries, from flight dynamics to the intricacies of modern security systems.

Each new project was an adventure, a testament to their unbreakable bond and mutual respect. Nana's unwavering belief in Man Man's potential fueled his confidence, while Man Man's curiosity and enthusiasm rekindled Nana's own sense of wonder.

Together, they built models, systems, and a foundation for an enduring partnership that celebrated the joy of learning and the power of dreams.

With each shared project, Nana and Man-Man discovered new dimensions of their relationship, building models and systems and a treasure trove of memories and mutual admiration.

They marveled at the intricacies of technology, from the mechanics of flight to the complexity of security Systems, and each exploration brought them closer.

Nana found joy in Man Man's unquenchable curiosity, while Man-Man thrived under Nana's unwavering encouragement.

Their bond, forged through patience, shared interests, and a willingness to learn from one another, transformed their understanding of family and partnership, creating a legacy that celebrated the boundless possibilities of dreams pursued together.

Driven by an insatiable thirst for knowledge, Nana embarked on a journey of aviation discovery under Man-Man's expert tutelage. They delved into the rich tapestry of aviation literature and captivating documentaries, Man-Man generously dispensing his encyclopedic understanding of aircraft designs and their complex mechanisms.

Their shared exploration evolved into a harmonious pursuit, each undertaking adding a vibrant page to their collaborative narrative. Nana's insightful guidance and unwavering support complemented Man-Man's infectious enthusiasm and inquisitive spirit, propelling them into uncharted territories of aeronautical understanding.

Their connection deepened with every shared success. Together, they mastered the intricacies of flight dynamics and the nuances of aviation security, constructing functional models and a treasure trove of cherished memories, a testament to their profound bond.

Their collaboration, forged in mutual esteem and a fervent passion for discovery, converted every obstacle into a catalyst for advancement and delight. This shared odyssey, a testament to the potency of teamwork and the exquisite blossoming of aspirations fostered by affection and empathy transcended mere professional achievement. Their exploration of aviation and security technologies became a profound expedition into the heart of their bond, revealing the intricate landscape of their evolving relationship.

Each project they undertook became a cornerstone of trust and admiration, with Nana learning to appreciate the intricacies of technology through Man-Man's eyes and
Man-Man drawing strength from Nana's unwavering belief in him.

Their collaboration transcended limitations, each breakthrough and conquered challenges fueling their shared exhilaration. This alliance, forged in the crucible of inquisitive minds, reciprocal admiration, and guiding mentorship culminated in an enduring heritage that ignited the imaginations of all who knew them. It served as a vibrant testament: with unwavering support and a boundless spirit of discovery, the potential isn't confined—it's merely the threshold of limitless horizons.

Nana's Airplane
Journey

Nana was awestruck by Man-Man's encyclopedic knowledge and fervent enthusiasm. He became her personal tutor, an expert guide into the captivating world of aviation, revealing the intricate mechanisms of those majestic flying machines.

Their collaborative endeavors extended to crafting detailed airplane models, fueling their shared aspiration of attending a thrilling air show or, even more wondrously, experiencing Nana, a pillar of unwavering support who was consistently astonished by Man Man's inventive brilliance and fervent dedication.

Conversely, Man Man flourished under her steadfast mentorship and insightful guidance. Their collaborative spirit transcended ordinary familial relationships, propelling them into a vibrant partnership. Each creation has extraordinary accomplishments. Their explorations became a source of profound satisfaction, and their shared triumphs cemented an indissoluble bond strengthened with every collaborative undertaking.

Nana's steadfast devotion and Man-Man's insatiable inquisitiveness formed a powerful partnership, a vibrant ecosystem where knowledge blossomed, and exploration thrived. Their collaborative efforts forged a deeper bond, propelling Man-Man's burgeoning passions to new heights.

Nana's heart overflowed with pride as she witnessed her grandson's self-assurance blossom, his aspirations taking wing with each revelation.

Together, they immersed themselves in workshops, museum expeditions, and community groups, showcasing Man-Man's exceptional abilities. Nana discovered she was not merely a caregiver, but a fellow learner, captivated by the extraordinary world her grandson was unveiling. Man-Man's confidence soared as he recognized his grandmother as a steadfast ally, a champion of his dreams, nurturing his insatiable curiosity.

Their shared journey transcended mere academics and technical pursuits; it was a tapestry woven with cherished memories, a legacy of profound respect and unwavering love destined to endure. Through every project and discovery, Nana and Man-Man embodied the transformative power of genuine connection and mutual understanding, a testament to the boundless inspiration that springs from such a bond.

A Twist in The Tale

Man-Man's latest fascination captivated Nana: security cameras.

His request revealed a burgeoning ingenuity. "I want to build my own security system," he declared, his voice brimming with enthusiasm.

Nana, ever supportive of his intellectual explorations, readily embraced the challenge. Their collaborative journey into home security was a testament to their shared passion.

Hours were dedicated to dissecting the mechanics of various camera types; Nana was consistently astounded by Man-Man's sharp intellect and technical aptitude resulted in a remarkably efficient and minimalist security apparatus, a testament to his boundless creativity. Man-Man's capacity for practical problem-solving and his relentless drive to refine the system left Nana profoundly impressed.

His potential shone brightly, solidifying her belief in his extraordinary abilities. Their technological forays became a cornerstone of their evolving relationship, fostering mutual admiration and shared ambitions. This shared journey ignited a powerful bond, promising a future with exciting possibilities and unparalleled discoveries.

Recognizing the brilliance inherent in his inventive nature, Nana wholeheartedly embraced Man Man's burgeoning passion. Their collaboration was immediate, a deep dive into the mechanics of photography, culminating in a customized darkroom setup within Man Man's own space. Nana was consistently astounded by Man Man's ingenious problem-solving and insatiable technical appetite.

Their shared exploration of aviation and security technologies transcended mere technological inquiry; it forged an unbreakable bond. Each undertaking served as a testament to their growing trust and mutual respect. Nana gained a profound appreciation for the intricacies of technology through Man Man's insightful lens, while Man Man thrived on Nana's unwavering faith in his abilities.

Together, they relentlessly pushed the boundaries of innovation, finding immense satisfaction in each creation and every challenge conquered. This partnership, a tapestry woven from inquisitive minds, expert guidance, and profound admiration became a beacon of inspiration, demonstrating that with nurturing support and a shared sense of awe, the possibilities extend far beyond the heavens, reaching into the infinite expanse of the unknown.

Beyond their domestic sphere, their joint endeavors
became a quest for intellectual expansion and global
awareness.
Nana pursued evening studies, diligently mastering
the technical intricacies of Man-Man's fervent
projects. Man-

Man, in turn, ravenously consumed every
piece of Knowledge, infusing his creations
with boundless ingenuity.
Their presence at technology expos and air
shows was magnetic to all who
encountered them.

Their exploits powerfully demonstrated the transformative effect of
shared knowledge across generations, showcasing the boundless
possibilities unlocked by fostering inquisitive minds and fervent
enthusiasm. Collaboratively, they forged not merely a collection of
endeavors, but a rich and enduring heritage, a
testament to ingenuity, affection,
and the unshakeable ties of
kinship.

Conclusion: Legacy of Support

Shared escapades among airplanes and cameras forged an unbreakable, affectionate connection between Nana and Man-Man. Nana came to cherish Man-Man's exceptional abilities and fervent interests, recognizing that fostering his passions would pave the way for a remarkable future. Their shared aspirations, soaring amongst the clouds and intricate contraptions, were fueled by Nana's unwavering encouragement, urging Man-Man to embrace audacious pursuits with unwavering courage.

Their explorations continued relentlessly, Nana and Man-Man perpetually seeking novel experiences to broaden their comprehension of the world. Excursions to aviation museums ignited Man-Man's spirit; his eyes blazed with wonder at the sight of legendary aircraft, while Nana reveled in his burgeoning expertise and infectious enthusiasm.

They found kindred spirits within a vibrant local technology club, a haven for individuals who passionately embraced innovation and lifelong learning. Each workshop and exhibition

became a testament to their shared dedication, reinforcing their profound bond and mutual inspiration.

Their dialogue deepened their connection, fostering Increasingly audacious aspirations. Nana's unwavering support and Man Man's insatiable inquisitiveness fueled their progress, forging a heritage destined to motivate themselves and future generations. This partnership Powerfully illustrated that with affection, collaborative effort, and a mutual thirst for discovery, obstacles crumble, and dreams blossom into tangible achievements.

Reflection

Nana's journey with her grandson, Man-Man, began amidst misunderstandings but blossomed into a shared pursuit of dreams. She discovered that nurturing young minds requires patience, empathy, and a collaborative spirit of mutual learning.

Their bond deepened as they embarked on exciting adventures in technology and innovation. Workshops became their classrooms, museums their playgrounds, and community clubs the stage for Man-Man's burgeoning talents.

Nana, in turn, found herself both a mentor and a fellow explorer in her grandson's captivating world.

His self-assurance soared as he experienced his grandmother's unwavering belief in his aspirations and enthusiastic encouragement of his inquisitiveness. Their shared endeavors transcended mere technical achievements; they forged enduring memories, a legacy of love and profound respect.

Each project and each discovery served as a powerful testament to the transformative potential of genuine connection and mutual understanding. Their collaborative spirit evolved into the very bedrock of their relationship, fostering intimacy and shared appreciation.

Whether attending cutting-edge tech expos or meticulously constructing airplane models, every activity reflected their unbreakable bond and insatiable curiosity.

They inspired each other to aim higher to envision greater possibilities. The true value of their journey resided not in the milestones reached but in the richness of their shared experiences. Became an inspiring example of intergenerational examples.

Their story illuminates the extraordinary power of collaborative partnerships, demonstrating the boundless potential unleashed when hearts and minds unite for a common purpose.

Index

- Man-Man's
  camera
  project
- Setting up cameras

    - Family

- Nana's stories
- Talking
  about
  family

    - Learning and Growing

    - Nana learning from Man-Man Dreams for the future

    - Nana is learning from Man-Man Dreams for the future

ABOUT THE AUTHOR

MARKEESHA PERRY, known affectionately as "Nana," is a gifted wordsmith, a weaver of intricate tales that deeply connect with diverse readers.

Her profound storytelling ability shines through works such as "The Tapestry of My Life," "How Keesha Survived the Ghetto," and "The Black Cloud that Cast No Shadow." These powerful narratives seamlessly blend Perry's personal experiences with a vibrant imagination, offering illuminating insights into the human spirit.

Central to Perry's writing is an unwavering exploration of resilience, familial bonds, and uplift, leaving an enduring mark on her readers.

Her distinctive voice, forged in the crucible of life's challenges, imbues her stories with both relatability and empowerment. Each carefully constructed sentence resonates with the strength she discovered while navigating life's complexities.

Keesha, {A.K.A.} NANA; emphasizes the critical importance of human connection and the timeless strength of love. Beyond the written word...

Perry finds joy in pursuing diverse passions and sharing adventures with her cherished family, a constant wellspring of inspiration fueling her creative endeavors.

Her parents, Linda, aka {lil Lin} and Frank, aka {Boldie}, are a testament to the enduring power of family and its influence on her remarkable journey.